# THE FORTY DAYS

Books by David McAleavey

Sterling 403

The Forty Days

# THE FORTY DAYS

David McAleavey

an Ithaca House book
Ithaca, N.Y.

Grateful acknowledgement is made to the editors of the following publications where several of these poems first appeared: *The First Anthology, Granite, Occurrence, Poetry, Rainy Day, Solstice,* and *Stone Drum Anthology.*

"A Sheaf of Light" and "Fire-Boned" first appeared in *Poetry*

ITHACA HOUSE, 108 North Plain Street, Ithaca, New York 14850

Ithaca House books are distributed by Serendipity Books 1790 Shattuck Avenue, Berkeley, California 94709

# CONTENTS

# CONTENTS (continued)

# AT CERTAIN OLDER

at certain older more sure & compressed depths
quarries are abandoned, the rock turned as useless
& as if spatially distant — as many quasars
away — as the universe is old, from which this
house.  & not just depths, but fish who run lit

gorge streams knocking fishermen wade — then
to open & find beggars, starved prayers, displayed,
offering — not Middle experience, not the hollow
under bell curve too small for *jive queens the
litt whisp "Mynherr! the distance!"* — who answer

the querent (what can be his?)  "a plastic sack
tied to the door's knocker appeared to contain
fresh smelt fillets dropped by Jim on his way
to Syracuse he caught in the gorge; & contained in
fact that smelt, fanned below the knot." this is

one way to make a living transposing elements
from nature, producing a carpet or blanket
colored by recent discoveries in photography
with last fall's leaves during this spring's melt,
soggy intricate snow-blotch islands over-

lapped browns redsorange yellow points in the mass,
reduced in size; or another, etching your own
yearning whimsy & grief deep within solomon's
shadow drawn with candleflame on the night
sky, the universe, as he admires sheba.

# A WOMAN DARNS

a woman darns thin green socks & tired, blinks.
but the mint held in a tumbler of water releases
such a smell of blue wind twined in the core
of each squared stem her eyelids open:
yes, blue wind. mint brings a need for sight.

sight: opening blink illumination distends
pores air enters, once on hollywood boulevard.
gleaming bubbles on the stream ride to falls. now
a spanish-olive-colored VW bus rolls by: she tries
to calculate what number of coinciding hours

bears possibly on that color bus juxtaposed
this noon on plain street with a tumbler of mint,
the hours leading to clarity — ideal zero becomes
the ache she takes for warmth, hunting her archer
in precariously drawn aim, held in the pergamon

as if buttressed into permanence against keen-
edged. . . but the pergamon bombed? only
in stillness does energy shine, give sound, draw
form in matter, deep-grilled matter! common pond,
deep calm joy. Hail, gunfire king whose lurch

is sight so clear the service ends. so chill
& steep a vision. she works to keep feet warm.
hunched, she works. the butterchurn? no, shivering,
everything is to be done, that is to be;
green things shine in soil the spade shined.

# WICHITA

wichita july sunsets brings families to
hear the honking musicians' union civic band
at the park. they drift off to the zoo & back
for sousa. mosquitoes, chiggers, chattering kids
hop in the sandbox, how many people there were.

before, the postcard shows golden gate
with no bridge. later, that is now. cinders
at sunset crater (flagstaff), marble bits
from pompeiian mosaics, all the floors feet
note: slime, tombstones awry, no road. no road.

what brings tears hardly loosens its hold, offers
advice: if the toilet pumps gas, give in & move.
do not read *The Principles of Economics* during
class. work at home, weep at home, divine
inner truth of at least one thing by dowsing.

& appearance: inside his watch the inscription
reads "deep thanks to Tom Blaiford whose service
to my sist" & then has worn off. outside
time is 4:02 PM, but that hardly matters to him
in Tom's life. practiced piano when he should.

let him. forget all the traffic tickets, whatever
your parents blamed you for. or blame the amoebas
caring for themselves as they do inside you, as
inside turning hubcaps the stillness is pointless.
do not object. underline even the billboards.

## ODORS FROM A JAR

odors from a jar; in the wind posters wave
on top of boxes, order relationships & wine
slurring together yesterday, today, the -apparat.
giant radiowave sending tubes, the -apparat.
above the posters drapes the plain green wall.

lilac leaves are opening, oak leaves large as
a kitten's ear, planting time. tulip trees bloom
& tulips & the hyacinths have already faded.
this week morels should show, other fungi
going; early peas begun inside vine. horoscopes

acknowledge that effectiveness of plans hinges
on receptivity in others; thus the special signs
fountains provide changing in little ways,
which soothes, seeing small things. entertaining
& comfortable they never repeat, since not

caught up in names. tomorrow a trip to vineyards
will come for someone. for someone will trip.
someone uses the future tense even when
today once never seemed possible. hope is
melodious until the tune is done. is done.

the lord's angel waits for a hookup, skirts
covering jordan. camping, & everything, is dear.
friends transmit offers, & remain friends. hard
up. no dinner tonight. dogtails spiral down stairs
as flesh twists & lolls all day around a flu.

# APPARENT HUMAN

after a drawing by Anita Siegel
*NY Times 22 IV 73*

apparent human figures scale a wall  inside
they busily congratulate another  other bodies
fall to fires or medieval kitchens inscribed
"thise cokes . . ." & stir the brew pots  what
clatter  sometimes trap doors lead to traps

of no comfort  nobody says "thing." along one
gallery swords & pincushions; gibsons confer
with tom & jerries; cold with fire  the onions
escaped or waiting lie in cellared bins.
Do not go in!  the door says, frightening.

the magnificent air holds brahms  brahms
holds a mirror  the mirror shows madonna
in her best light, a light green frock
fluted in an italian manner  the motorcycle
carries a baby harness  baby is in.

from skyscrapers objects which seem human
pop  behind brahms a noise hunts company.
no relief in subways tho they hump & weep,
at the end of the tunnel is light  the light
shrieking your name no friend, in no friend's

tongue  the upper left corner, handsome, embossed,
reveals pastoral settings  several young men
tend a garden  lots of hoes & baskets now full
with lettuce, tomatoes, beets  in the background
cucumber beetles dance the squash bugs' tune.

## NOT A WALK

not a walk by water but water *solus,* pushed
high above the metamorphic bed, settling faster,
little "force" to contradict— "force," friction,
the impossible gnash of nightmare amphibians. . .
— & not only formed as by a jar, but scraping

the earth fault after fault, tormented
tosses where it works, tosses, lies.
the darkest tremblings inside sewers, rivers
vanish in sand. in caverns of every size
stalagmites form nearly past the grip of time

— one drop in your life, young brontosauri
splashed in the shallows down a few feet ago,
no guarded life. what if you now often see
calm pools, have clear vision or courage blank
as granite in the surf, ferocity like the surf

growling at the granite? or flow, undertow.
serene, skiing on the highest mountains,
everything slopes away: the beauties of being.
a special point, *flatness:* no opposition,
no tricks of perspective. so you have reached

the falls, lie calm in the mouth, your head
lifts out at the lip & only panorama holds you.
your fall is graceful; turning over & over
everything changes. you dig a hole
at the end, & spray floats in the valley.

# THERE IS A HEAD

there is a head in the flour sack
maneating panthers crouch on truck roofs
dark spots on the floor open & close
brakes squealing outside, compressed skulls
things are linked:  under the final kleenex

a poem issues directions for burial:
in a swamp under sputtering stones.
watch dogs bark at mice where burglars
carry sten guns.  drinking water you shine
in the bluish light as car-size tarantulas

climb down the slope of the roof.  if the roof
collapses call it "luck," an easy escape
from terror.  door panes shatter & assault rifles
spray whatever moves, moved, might have.
kitchen knives disappear from the drawer day by day

& moans multiply by the window.  a horse's head.
on the seat you take in the bus is a book
detailing, like the Warren Report, your murder;
no help if it lies or dismisses a second murderer,
it shows you wearing the lilac shirt you love.

postage stamps gummed with poison, radio-
active medallions scrambling neurons— when you see
green broccoli you hug yourself in a blanket.
the blanket itches, remember?  pull the cord
& the ceiling falls, you looking for your fate.

# STREET, SIDEWALK

street, sidewalk, window. the oak's buds
hunch up from the business below. still tight.
they grow into sudden expansion & then great size
hard & slow at first like balloons. they come from
a lot. dust sticks to the window, shows the rain.

"tender jurisprudence, the phil silvers kilowatt
revue begs" (carrot intersection of caco-
phony boulevard— whoever believed; whoever
uncovers a fascination with the typewriter's k:
a kiev of knickerbockers, kingfishers, kon—

no justice, do not pretend there is justice,
let young ones shove, resign yourself
to the chromatograph your older age is. pylons,
tiglath-pileser, thruway bridges & underducts
of quarries, fissures, castiron bullhorns

humming Behemoth Behemoth, so many cycles a second,
would that mask. . .). jot: find the right note:
his final no-hitter. behemoth that hates us,
fixture nitpickers georgian escape, horizon,
mastodon. dust shows the rain. in music,

accidentals. mannikins, DO not drop a stitch.
joined across so much water two such "towns"
collided. in a month the dozen brown leaves
skirring in the wind will not matter, or vanish;
or that they are oaks, or withered & torn.

# PERFECT RASCALS

perfect rascals thieve, beside bastards, fewer
of the meek animals of america who ordain
"no dogshit on our lawns." there are other
targets: stocks, rye distilleries, restroom lock
manufacturing. industrial parks near every city

breathe in captains, laboring men to trim
hydrangeas. men trim the shrubs to keep them
back. cut, they keep back, in exchange
while early in the morning hydrangea bushes
noiselessly; in evening's hollow even fewer

acts of reason. dogs dream, we halloa.
the park surrenders to haze, so the sunshine
amounted to an address in a suburb,
flowers, trees, eggs cooking on a tin can
hobo stove. baseball. golf. the laws ordain

no man master tho option rests light
on the few unfailing. truly the laws rest,
everything sets quite ordinarily still, even light
is still. this is cold: flowers, distilleries, oil
refineries make for an ambience, the target

of argument & tower of prose. stephen proton.
horror of faces, hooked in the jaw, elbows
depressed & stained by grass— a sonata
evening revealed the lack, monotonal lock
two three four of every mugger in the city.

# WHAT HAS THE ROUTE MONEY

what has the route money to do with it?  what about
the albatross, the double bind speaking without
moving his lips?  why *is* the dam useless, the flood
"empty of love," the house "sweeping streets like
a squeegee"?  why must every murder end in nothing?

when the car stalls in water, what pleasures
appear unasked in the imagination?  was it too hard
to answer?  which doctor shines lights in your eyes,
which percusses your chest?  when will the price
of barnswallows affect children dreaming about

unspoiled forests, virgin prairies, gold teeth?
how about children dreaming they can vote, teach
class, have religion?  what got into her, stuffing
kleenex into her underpants on the sand pile?
who was dr. fabrique before he came to town?

was he a pimp?  could he have been yesterday?
will the town buzz?  if sudden noise alarms you
must you always turn & return to dying?
what in any case did the witching owl mean
by "dropping consciousness below the level of

death," inking every resolve in the same trauma?
how can a stratofortress bomb asia & the same night
moan in your dream, newspapers twisting in air
as the days turn?  how will you choose one
harmonious refrain from the melodies of sand?

# FINALLY NOUGAT

finally nougat is added, and this tube contains
jolts, lightning flashes, fortifications against
jerusalem, pinot noir to the contrary, jewels
do not grow in glass, but there is the harmony
of guests dipping their fingers in wine & rimming

their glasses, each posting a signal: & each glass
unique, clinging to the hillside of sound
coiled in your head as ocean clings to the hills
of the ocean floor, the mariana trench, & storms.
beneath the trenches, junk, paraphernalia, beads.

what the tube contains comes at you full of sweets
nourishing every shredded difference between fact
& the illuminations of fact in retrospect, kept
lively by phanopoeia & desertion, tempered between
tremendous discharge & stupendous need, equalled

only by walls in mirrors, wine in the ponds,
a dying maraschino suckling at the glass while
emphatic & deranged devotees lunge keel-less
at bait strung for featherweight fish groping
for warmth with the bit of gristle, & journey

pool to pool seeking true takes of the unknown,
the original *NYTimes* Sunday Crossword Puzzle;
as for walls in the mirrors, acknowledge the space
around you, acknowledge the mars heard on records
made by echo fed back through always fading glass.

## DRUNKEN ATTACKS

drunken attacks, bitter rue: disengagement
rather than duels: shame & tired eyes; the overcast
breaks, but no escape, & continual suspense
until the cops catch up is felt as fear, fear
streamlines into boredom which then inherits

its own terror growing with each new break.
work in the belief that matter can be worked
into conclusion; tho only minor problems end;
but no end of rue: which nearly balances this
growing argument coming to need longer pointing

starting over from a different beginning; meanwhile
association compels argument to become a pencil,
scribbling at the guilt over incautious drunken
talk, & the boredom, & terror, wanting to write
enough to do the impossible taking back, redoing:

& needing to be sharpened: which is as far as
association goes, leaving logic to complete
the tactics of argument. there is no way to ignore
such weight on your mind. every out that might
excite those electrons to a new energy level is

merely ideal, the pleasure of maybe getting
away with it corrupts to terror, & chaos claims
terror not when the job is "finished," & only
arbitrarily when you quit your work, & if death
is more than a knot on a string, only then.

*for* William J. Harris

## FLETCHED & VARNISHED

fletched & varnished, the shaft dries. the head
is pointed, the wrappings ready. heris on the floor
move in a draft. twisted gut slumps around the bow
in the corner. fingers twitch, press the thumb
the way they curl drawing aim; glue hardens & cracks.

sauce slowly thickens in the pot. carrot peels
stand in a pile on the garbage disposal cover,
onion skins, roots. the dog who got meat trimmings
sleeps by the stove. tomato juice seeps into
the cutting board. tarragon spills from a jar.

the heads torqued back, covers on, valves adjusted;
the oil pump gears replaced, & a new gasket, only
the plate to tighten, connect the wires, add oil
& check for drippage from the main seal.
sockets & box ends lean against the tires.

the white knight forks queen & rook; a black
bishop threatens knight, pawn, king; centerboard
is a jungle. each side has taken pawns & knight,
which stand by the ashtray. white removes bifocals
& sets them by the cigarettes. black sips coffee.

poised for the future, preparation's traces as plain
evidence as talus, the plainest statement
of probability, a new factory gearing for tomorrow's
production, speaker walking to the podium, ordered
notes in hand beginning "on the way here today."

# AT THE BIRTHDAY

at the birthday party everyone got a favor
addressed usually to a school, heidelberg,
berkeley, alphabetized & taped on the wall.
sometimes the clue was more particular (classics,
ag economics); sometimes the favor awaited a name.

after dinner the party moved outside in order to
walk to the place where the party would really
start. in the suburbs, in the fresh snow,
the course was confused, & a few professors'
lawns were trampled. finally they put up a sign:

Go Down This Road to the End. in places so many
have made the path icy, & sliding seems best.
the rises are difficult & a dwarf gets ahead
around the flank. finally the group enters a valley
& climbs onto a high mesa, where camp has been

struck: rows of two-man tents. one huge flap
of canvas is the party tent the party itself
must raise. everyone gets busy. back home,
the family quarrels about heat, & father reads
the newspapers in an outer unheated bedroom.

inside the big tent among five thousand people,
one famous young poet holds hands with another
whose face looks like the photo on his new book,
which he holds up by his face. is that so?
someone asks, if that is so then this is winter.

# NIGHT. —

night. — new birch leaves shove each other
making a flickering blanket of light, lightweight—
in a seersucker jacket a car salesman shouts
preaching tolerance, "real" love, competition:
very cool to skin, easily laundered (leave it out

in the rain!), also use this new sleeping aid
for a sunshade! it's fireproof! doubles as a metro-
nome! — inky caps collapse, deliquesced, in a puddle
of spores on the windowsill; cooked they lapse
into ink & a bit of neutral-colored flesh.

— next door the old folks watch a rerun,
johnny weismuller as tarzan, swimming
to rescue jane as fast as his enemy
navigates the bank. faster, since tarzan wins.
— plastic sixpack halters lie near the fence.

empty cans. cars go by dragging mufflers, other
folks go by dragging cars from stopsign to light.
— across the street in the movie house sex
fantasies unwind, familiar, unfamiliar, labelled "x"
as if to mark a distinction, tho in every case some

one seems to do something better than someone else
in this tarzanest of worlds. the old folks
remember. living in the mountains old men in japan
eat *aduki* beans, waiting to die like the deer
in jeffers' poem, or the poet in *alastor*

## GENIUS, FAT WOMAN

genius, fat woman, preside, gnaw caves out from
within hardest grief, star the insides of every
chamber where the rock drill churns, with interlace.
let names be spelled with powder, let the wind blow.
make cause be triumphant, have effect follow.

do not limit causes for one effect, nor effects
from one cause. be fair. have it so all in all
no system is supreme. but remove grief, each bite
fouler than the first, from inside, with grace.
decorate every temple to beauty with a frieze,

The Defeat of Reason by Inadequate Means, Genius
Tyrannus. always praise yourself this way
for the sake of everyman. screw in public windows
& let it appear as a vase of flowers on a soggy bed.
the flowers should be myrtle, but every pretender

should be misled by a series of seemingly arcane
scribbles into seeing the myrtle as essential
barbed wire, pine trees at each essential barb
pointing any way. let scales slide, & flutes
become a bother. if there must be harmony have it

feature nothing but the vlop-vlop-vlop of hard shoes
on a sidewalk. let the land come in as far as the
sea. create magnets that bake bread, & compasses
that wake you regularly at 7:00. O genius, preside,
put circles inside squares until you go through.

## IF IT WAS ALWAYS

if it was always flowers flowers would not hurt
the way lilacs hurt, or each & every tulip
petal making its way through rain, true to
the beat of its own suppleness, or showing power
in humility grow; if rain did not break flowers,

or if goats did not butt, or you had no need to lay
a blanket on the goat, or superimpose on any image
a goat under a blanket reaching for a clump
of violets, its mouth twisted & ready to close
like pliers with a worn hinge, grating teeth. . .

here the diver is poised, the breeze coming up
from the pool. everything hovers. his eyes sting
looking; it is all so beautiful; the world is
in his eyes turquoise, white marble; he dives.
words pursue him: asphodel, goatdance, pentagraph.

but downcast the woman mature, no longer girl,
walks beside the construction barricade, eyes
on bits of glass, dirt, the few weeds quick
enough to sprout in any unused area, poisoned
by auto exhaust, dying yellow on the asphalt.

surely everyone sees that words are not enough
to keep her, that words must be said over & over &
eventually people are happy to avoid translation
or any extra labor, letting the words fall in time
to the beating tulips, petals on the grass.

# A SHEAF OF LIGHT

a sheaf of light speaking centimeters off
the story of flood, the story of death, the story
misery knows, the grand story of delusion & bliss,
speaking turtle posture, ostrich technique, beaver
message; or the story of grace, halo, possibility;

speaking miles off, using beacons & farsighted
observers, speaking into iron vats kilometers
apart, & into flaming indian paintbrush,
spirea bushes, into giant clams, savings banks;
a sheaf of orange light, coral light, blonde

highlights. ultimately sheaf of light, of grain,
of arrows, of grain held in an arrow's wood,
& the sheaf matter is, hollow-hard, uncolored
glowing. in any one place, any circumference, on
any map that shows the gleaming place it speaks.

it says come together. it says diverge. it says
everything except darkness which merely says "ah,"
ghosting along the channels of light; behind every
speech non-speech, every message falls on silence;
it says beauty, irish comfort, no death but in life,

& no life there; says pomegranate, every fruit
in season, every season; complete instant union,
undecipherable gap between things, & every possible
relative position; the sheaf speaks such a clear
warning, clear as a bundle of light in your hand.

*for* A. R. Ammons

# TAKEN FROM GOLDER'S

taken from golder's green to a guilder's zee, mumb-
ling, stumped, stunted by that question, what hand-
book on this new poetic "heat sky hot evening";
"froggy jewels bored her in the out the of from";
"the cutter's position, above trade, beyond money";

also "natural suspect lemon that being moldy";
and "says she's fuckable, says don't pick one up."
in this channel passage soggy bees & slugs in beer
touch *la poeme anti-mechanique*, manichean brats,
*leurs largesses.* now bees go slow, slugs soon die.

thriving trilliums, coltsfoot, uncurling ferns
red baneberry, toothwort, jack-in-the-pulpit,
fish swatting at the sky on account of the flies
buzzing on their ceiling, blood tracks on acoustic
tile, their mark sounding splash in air.

liveliness in this fresh air, & you become
confident, you refuse to have tea, you say london
england, descartes, amsterdam holland, california.
mechanical plants seem slower, so few blooms fade;
tho each husk loosens too fast & grim to see

without clenching like trees clench sidewalks
or grab the cliff they help to break; the hand-
book says let language fuel you, that is
your chief client & connector of enterprise while
you strike interfaces, curve by a lemon, disarray.

## COME CLOSER

come closer. think what a leprechaun is, only
an inner-movie-screen size human figure frolicking
at the base of an oak tree, tough barked, brown-
gray. elves are larger, probably spawned by
a shortsighted race of humans. do not be short-

sighted: come closer. phantoms rise towards you
in your dreams and fall back, away, swallowed back
to blackness; they never come to you alive, life-
size, tho you wait for them & wait, you can only
come closer, smaller, increasingly to resemble

a leprechaun: so *come* closer, *hear* closer, hear
ice forming, corn growing. a tiny man could stub
his toe in a salt shaker cap, an old gopher hole
is his cave, & what you call a cavern is another
universe, the damp mineral roof speckled like

the sky of hell. cautious politic gestures may seem
necessary, but only frolicking acts of probity will
survive to greet you: honor is practiced; a primary
entertainment is discussing universals, non-random
modes of abstract thought or lovingkindness. come

closer. energy you store shrinking is yours,
it comes back to you; it need not make you happy
since it is only the difference life makes, but
think what man you could make with your breath
& some clay, how you could make him happy. come.

# THE CURTAIN

the curtain trembles, holding the shower.
tomato & dill seeds sprouting, in a vase
a cherry bough flowers; persistent use of anti-
histamines may cause kidney trouble, tree flowers
take lots of water, parochial school underway at 8.

avoid too much reliance on the symbols of thought,
seek thought enough.—   swallows swoop in the gorge.
—   "nixon believed involved," sources sprout gurgling
"out of holes in the story fresh leaks spring."
talk of two possible meanings is closed to

a possible regression of meanings.  sink hooks
into what rises but freely cast for better:
don't be afraid of being beholden, an old music
is better than none.  you entered a house
& walked till you seemed lost: former landmarks

change, sometimes the land— mountains turn
into valleys, buildings burn, trees disappear
altogether.  yet it is still the same house
no doubt decorated in the peculiar tastes
of the former tenants, including several amateur

interior decorators, honest-to-god priests of
several faiths, garbagemen.  if the seasons seem to
change a lot, you may be too far from earth.  syntax
believe it needs frequent change; since, hence
langland, "grammar is the ground of all our good."

## IT WANTS

it wants to get out. here it is frustrated
by the walls of channels. wealth will not
restrain it, everything seems to volunteer to be
a drain unless done in the "right spirit." amen.
even were that a drain it goes on wriggling,

hammering breath into form, & beating on the walls
of words always wants out. do not lose it! they say,
follow that serpent with your thumb on its throat.
be there, let it out even, calm, make it glow.
perhaps a fiery serpent seems inapt for the task

perhaps the task is unclear. the serpent is
proud, forthright as it gathers strength whenever
it's forgotten, prepares to march across frontiers,
does, devours new forests with concentrated mind,
firebrand, outlaw. it crosses into unfamiliarity

& offends some; but if you let it go only where
you're comfortable, that's dull: kick it hard.
inside the serpent a sea is writhing, & the serpent
tries to ride it, troubled by drowsiness, woozy
& tormented enough for a hero. enduring pain

is endurance: learn to kick holes in walls yourself
for it, keep it moving, not held back, like water
it has to flow & will notwithstanding. it can come
in torrents, water does, & drop great heights,
crashing at the bottom & breaking bloody into ocean.

## THAT THE CONVEYOR

that the conveyor moves is obvious:  the body
supine on the belt nears the saw.  the large
bandsaw "waits" for the body that is moving head-
first.  the eyes are closed, the hair short.  does
*ivory* "describe" it?  not really, because the head

splits into red falling open like a log would.
a twelve-year-old yelling SCUZ!  SCUZZY!  points at
flowervases, & the imp grins!  every vase turns
to algae, & stagnation, spanish moss, & cypress
picking up its feet from the water (picking its

feet from the beats of water, turning, picking
the beats.  this is the base of rock bands energizing
millions, watery names, own devils).  the flowers
wilt & yield to a green mold, "idiot's laughter."
the pre-teen wins friends easily.  a pendulum swings

in the same plane telling twenty-four hours a day,
travelling a time circle, across the table a coat
of leather dries on a chair.  the circle swings.
that steady sound is no refrigerator, not tractor-
trailers on the highway or the slow full rain of

new york state; & not the sound of a pendulum
floating on its bearings.  the distant sound is *saw.*
& the body moves, supine, head-first, into it.
this goes slowly; blood sprays, gore coats the *saw.*
head half-sliced, everything goes to blackness.

## SUCH A CRAZY

such a crazy placekick, to scuttle under the home
team's bench. all detail of subterfuge knocked
into history. history of the dullest kind, things
actions smooch up to. olive oil president shakes
every candidate's tree with his back hand. what a

grip! cheerios hold their form as well or better,
engineering works. the ugliest most hateful
connections, the grimace that wishes you unborn,
smells your corpse inside your skin. checkers
for such a person are clean, as if inferred from

an absence of smell. cannot the worst be said?
after all, light diffracts through every layer
& is not so changed. no. land's end thrashes
in the sea but none can say so, or say so worst.
a trace of a touch remains, words drill back down

to nothing but keep it from you. refracted light
certainly shows prisms, even in the video room.
engineering works, embarrassment not. vacationers
note the seaweed, the mosquitoes, the dead sea
lion swarming with flies, voices declare

to the back of the head "they won't bear it,"
three virgins in the bed together, flanks tight.
the plants are coming up all right in the spring.
plastic soap uncovers without cleaning. happily
it was the last carton; so many breasts examined.

# SITTING ON A BENCH

sitting on a bench an old man barks at a pigeon.
the pigeon squawks & strides away.  a girl walks by
& tells him better ways to feed birds & pass time
but when he thinks of time it is water nearly run
from a pool, each drop a long reverberation,

& his eyes cringe. his signature has fallen near
total disintegration, his driver's license denied.
he doesn't want the girl to leave him, so much
like an old flame, so disjunct.  his face closes
behind emotion, tho he is tired, not rigid;

his eyes show greed; he yells across the park
when the sun comes clear of cloud, hits a stick
on the bench.  each thin blow kicks the drops:
sensations streamed toward him like rockets
when he was younger; he had no special theories;

if he caught fish he showed them around, & said
what people said:  he "regretted" the loss of wife
& child.  once like tilted pools rockets poured
on him confusing any thirst or insurrection; then
fire was kindleburst & now only these jerky pops

long into night.  sucking candy to sweeten her view
she tells him rare names, the chimeras, asks if
before he dies quetzlcoatl might come, flaxen hair
invisible in sunlight, his breath like paper, to
inscribe each final drop with texts from the dead.

## A GLITTERING

a glittering 1940's vocabulary, motion picture
house decor of the twenties, button collections
& rudimentary jazz recordings with three canaries,
a flugelhorn & a one-leg monkey in the traps to
scratch the brushes & thump the bass. everywhere

debris samples: a canvas scrap from the uffizi,
charred boards of the first white house. corroded
boxes reputed to have sunk in a galleon's hold.
childhood a recent time with an attic of antique
games, a closetful of war uniforms, an old

phonograph broken once when carrying the tune
of jim crack' corn, he doan care, massah's gone
to town. talk of a time of freedom, unusable
as a busted light bulb but free free from judgment.
*"they're dancing at the pond tonight darling"* —

underneath all this truth remains what sons accept
shaking hands with fathers at the depot, being set
not free but into limits, & the limit of language
always the first reached tho they still shake each
other gently. they would eat any surviving

passenger pigeon for farewell. both once looked
into the doll's mirror in the old doll house,
got down on hands & knees & crawled in the attic
to find themselves very small & close to the floor
at one end of a frightened, manumitted gaze.

# LILACS ARE

lilacs are most intense before the buds fully open.
later, fading in the sun, a brown clutch withers
them starting from the petal tips.  one bough
varies between prom pink & apple core brown.
the leaves are chicken hearts, tops, but green

& curling, wavy along the edges, thin, veined,
not possibly two-dimensioned.  one side is glossy
& a darker green than the underside carrying
the veins out of way like wood backing stage sets.
inside each cluster of flowers are a few small

leaves, perhaps to be there after the flowers have
blown. — well, she asks, so what? — these leaves
are small, & not easy to notice. — So what?  & why
this woodchuck skull?  everyone's got a skull. —
Just to be witness to one that once was:  when

she moves to stand petals fall on her bare legs;
when she stands petals fall to the floor, doubly
fallen — "hearing music like this makes you get so
sad." — composed she stands & composed petals fall.
her skin sheds, echoes renew her: echoes her body

makes remaking herself, echoes the petals make.
the pincushion when you puff the head off a
dandelion has holes at the regular intersections
of identically curved arcs, a pattern showing each
way.  due to parallax the moon can seem many places.

## HELLO JOURNEY ANGEL

hello journey angel poise patterning the backlands!
after today's study in and outdoors to be sitting
at night on a second floor facing east, a barren
situation to open, the world brought to a dark gray
& a few skeletal buildings twirling on towards

sun, the smith of vision, apollo, clear eyes.
father who does not know what love is, mother too
scared to show. so the family dog barks all day,
the neighbor's right to say goddamn sonofabitch.
the dog barks all day, sleeps out in the snow. a

hush happens, & hello journey angel poise! hardass
ways of feeling turn obsolete, sere, going toward
the sun what little difference facing east is &
seeming to fall backwards into space, or the other
way, riding to the future. if it is not music

that reaches here why are you suddenly silent?
water springs from the earth & flows east or west
following laws of chance & necessity, twins
doomed from the start, one bound never to live
the other quick to die. hello, poise!

poise that dances in trying to dance to this
heavenly music bleaker than the wall after death
swarming with snakes the Wanderer saw; & dancing,
looks gloom in the eye that dancing shines
on the woeful dog barking, long beyond love.

# SEIZED BY THE THROAT

seized by the throat the rattler cannot speak
her whole-bodied voice, has to scream "so long
fucker" with only a fury's fire to guide her, no
rhythm at all, only blind jerking behind a noose,
eye still & wild beyond pity, "fucker, so long,"

hard to have kept to such a thing & never seen the
wilderness beyond pity, if it comes down to that,
gut hollow pride that *commands* "Defend," in some
species more than others, in some cases more
or less strongly.  but if only the noose weren't

there!  the fangs would slink back in, to a cool
sneer. . . .  falcons can be too wild to eat im human
presence, a canada goose hiss dogs out of the
kitchen, the dogs hopelessly beyond recall, shame-
less & loving, & rabbits too stupid to care: in

all, only one face in a sneer, a knife in the back
on any suburban street, slicing like bats
in the dusk, intensification of gray; of
course the noose is there & the snake will die—
justice will not occur, for there is no model;

cars will police the streets, cultures will love
france, or france & england, hate arabs or chinese,
cold shoes may seem marzipan in an awful gesture
delimiting chaos. hard to know what you cleaved to,
hard to kill (you do) what you won't let speak.

drunk the conductor directs eyes open to different
widths to a few friends in the crowd. it strains
him, talking every day, persuading— so he's angry,
drunk, & "nobody's gonna spoil this goodtime,"
neighbor, not a penny, not vindication, not direct

challenge; even timidity can be wise in this game:
"the move really is anticipatory. since the danger
is lessened, black is in a better position to
threaten to capture the king pawn." chals marry
chis. debaters ask Is prophecy a temptation to be

cast down in the wilderness, or a rod raised by
thinking "to separate form & content is to falsify,
tho they are not the same & grow from each other;"
always there is tension is tension is always there.
the prophet preaches to show what he sees, that

any man who listens to another man instead of
god within loses all honor, or dies. that truth
is impartial, a plumbline shows faults. to feed
rock to water, water to fire. not to temporize
because you are young. to whip innocents with a

lash cured when the guilty cried. consider wrinkles
as the air does that erodes mountains. make
bridges no safer than ball bearings hold, make
lambs appear each spring, espouse the heroic ideal,
take no change for permanence, give only the past.

# KNOWING THE RANGE

knowing the range somewhat better he tried to help
whenever he could without building every fire
& taking every sighting; but being useful turned
him back onto his own most familiar pasture for
every pleasure, it did not ease him into the group

as he had hoped. his motives were profitless. his
goals however looked fine, at least no one seemed
to care to curtail him directly: if he wanted
to twirl the knobs on the coleman stove someone
would always remove the cylinder of gas. when they

sleep, he peers around the fire to see who are in
each bag. then they crown him king of the fest,
& he feels tragedy starting to brew intrigues
for him to swallow; then he asks what he did wrong
in so brief a term, admits paranoia. relieved,

he hears faint songs kept down throat before, &
chords. the fest spreads on, addictive, he will not
lead his group away as they pull him forward, can
he, "you know so much you could solve the sphinx."
he chooses a tree to climb, & holds to it warmly.

# CLOUD ANTELOPE

cloud antelope to fish mouth to paddlewheeler to
paddlewheel to swan, & then hibachi to potato chip
to birds touching wings to ketchup bottle, & otter
to kerosene lamp to valentine to turtle to globe
& on to butterfly, blimp, giant nose, pyramid.

in the pyramid one choice: the lower path sinks
like a knife-wound to darkness, the cold dry wind
stirred by the dragon's tail.  the half-man dragon
sleeps in his maze, his coils embracing chaos,
well-defended. every theseus renews him. upstairs

a woman steps from the shower into mirrors'
ricochet: with greater agility in that rare air
more can be seen (& with *your* refined eye!)
— poems lie thoughtless as leaves & just as common
along each path, scuffed to the sides by recent

passers-by. when you bring yourself to this sight,
what they might say makes no matter, each appointed
to one stage of reflection as a relief from mirrors;
most claim truth but truth is vision deferring;
tho she *could* be real, pyramid to bone to woman.

# AFTER RAIN

after rain the dogwood flower returns a kiss
with cool drops.  that is fine, you say, & ruffle
the spirea; a bird flutters down off her nest.
that is nice, you say, fresh eggs for dinner.
the bird goes out in your hand.  anesthesia, you

add, can come have dinner whenever she wants to,
with her insatiable desire for pain. the moon is
a yellow gourd in this weather. you say water! what
animals drink from it! very tall giraffes gather
in a circle & dunk their tongues. pardon, you say,

please don't go so away, leave the veldt out!
& nudge one car after another with your bumper.
suppose, you say in changing the subject, there
had never been any dodos in mauritius, would wild
geraniums have become an important protein source?

there having been dead birds before it is not
likely wild geraniums will be much investigated
by nutritionists. you accept this response in order
to clarify yours, that a good rain is a political
act of the highest stature, elements engaged.

## THESE POEMS

these poems wish to include little if any double-
talk since everything to be known can be known
simply, without logical process that lives in sub-
divisions. occasionally of course a dummy speaks,
or a series of dummies, beginning with the smallest

less than a robin's egg whose anxious face carved
in a knot screams misery. the next larger grins
like a golf ball because it's been hit so bad, & in
whom the lesser voice flames, a tumor, with rage.
this one will bear it till his cover fails &

worm-like rubber comes out. the hollow third dummy
floats in a bathtub: inside, the golf ball rolls
from skull to heels, fighting its pain, but the
third dummy just changes position, stretches,
scoops bubbles on his chest while his outfit dries.

the fourth dummy is roomsize, listening like blank
walls to the splashing. it looks from outside like
a window. the fifth dummy is a dead elm overreaching
the room, twigs scraping in wind; every other voice
a chainsaw piece-fitting the roof with vengeance.

# TEXTBOOKS

textbooks are the worst, proliferation of textbooks
is slightly better, with encouraged opposition. as
"poem" signifies you can't think over the music,
you give the music credit. be practical. if he says
"mulish & puling, the boys pile into each other," &

you try to separate them, you will consort nightly
with shins of bruises. figure to kill ants or hike
a long hill in your dreams, a long hill of satin.
the blue bandana picks its ass off the floor &
spins into *valse*, not every lover is tormented

by automotion. not every entry merits attention,
for instance conceiving a best way to grab lamps
lurching toward you. from the top are vistas more
impressive than beauty. land has tides too, turns
of rock & decay; & the globe part freezes, thaws

to be able to support oxidation & warm vegetation.
do not forget the anything that could have been
instead of this, even tho the large grievances that
make wars may have gone too far by now, & under-
standing each other come to seem too important.

# JUST SIT BACK

just sit back & think what you really want to say
now, in your heart's youth, to the world still
dimly imagined.  that you prefer such-and-such tea?
no, think why you sat back, overcome with grief.
to savor your own strength in surviving loss?  no?

out of loneliness then that can go to madness
seeking company?  because Futility carves his name
into everything you have done without him?  & death
becomes the bitter teacher of love, not life?
yes.  you sat back thinking what you have to say.

nearly anything could happen tho the unsaid comes
to nothing; & it seems important to say there is
nothing very important to be said; no world needs
to be mirrored, only to be augmented & kept from
shrinking.  & so if you can you will build poems

detailed as shrines & calm as sunflowers.  you have
to, but by no plan; were you forced to make a new
music?  or to see more clearly or to startle or to
ask for pity or cause to love?  you could have been.
you could have sat back just looking at your face.

# THE NIGHT EDITOR

the night editor pauses to clean his spectacles
for the sixth time, to unblur the characters he
proofs. each yawn is more profound than the last.
characters! he tells himself, same as bags of
rotten peaches. he throws some around. if *he* dozes

what can go right? who else will supervise a bound
tornado? it being crackerjack time. so long oh, he
adds, ohsolong (the battleship d. rivera at ten).
speak like an airhammer. be there, heard, now.
the violet radiation; extra coronal thrombosis.

when the night editor retires a watchman takes over
the guardianship of order, & under his rule it
gets no larger, nor does it shrink appreciably.
this is Grand Old Emotions Day, and fifteen dawn
horses are in a cage with a sabretooth who finally

reflects on how good the old days were. a critical
assumption, that literature doesn't change, is like
trying to hold a path but refusing its meditation
as too rigid. smoke seems to curl around the edges
of the paper, melpomene. & bring the acorn now.

# FROM SOME CHANNELS

from some channels the information is jumbled
& the picture itself hazy & only for a second
or two wholly recognizable. then it is clear
those channels too bear on the same matter, or at
least some part of it, as the normal channels of

being hurt when snubbed for instance, or feeling
that this week surely too many chores came your
way. often it is only the hazy channels that carry
the shows you want to see, & one result has been
an interest in magic & astrology, modes that try

to clarify (simplify) ambiguity. if a wall has two
sides two men stand on them listening to the other
listen to him, each with stethoscopes. inside
each ear the ringing gets louder until squirming
they twist themselves into deep puddles of spores

once alive. only once: the clearest messages are
often the most confusing, because clarity is
too painful to watch regularly. you try some
other plot offering suspense, romance, coffee
by the potful, then thirty years' bitter brooding.

# INSIDE THE HOUSE

inside the house built with twelve-inch studs
an old grandfather makes pizza, whirling
& pulling at the skin to make it uniform.
he hums to himself "every day the spider weaves
every day the frogs eat." he intends the chant

to relieve his boredom with forming new skins,
that disappears when each one nearly finished
is ready for his skill to bring any remaining
thickness or toughness down to the same plane
& twirl one last & nearly perfect turn in the air

before settling under the growing weight
of sauce, cheese, whatever. beauty does not demand
such close-spaced studs, or that the wood's
measure be full; or the modernist 16-inchers
now giving way to post-modern 24-to-centers, which

in fact means walls amount to less now. beauty shows
in the thinning skin the old man works, every
displeasing node of dough pulled into youthful
resilience, glossy with oil, not yet dulled by
flour, spinning above his hands in the old kitchen.

# FIRE-BONED

fire-boned the falls withstands its own weight
& speed, steaming out at the bottom to gloss
the gorge walls & the willows leaning into its cold
wind, their leaves wishing up, out, away from so
much damp, back west to sunset & the more stately

grove by the creek; even such an eden would have no
place for the revelations of abstract force the
falls makes, or the willows themselves twisted two
ways besides the tropisms conflicting to make order.
there is no need in eden for less than speaking a

matter straight off without evasion or repetition,
were there even any language suited to its nobility,
with perfect posture & deep even breathing.  still,
never to waver from a forward rush balancing time &
space is what the falls does; to canoe white water

finally demands more control than is possible, for
the falls are compelling; & flood opens out onto a
graceful incomprehensible delirium kept unexamined
by a mind preoccupied with its own safety, obsessed
with unity— peel twisting off its fiery skull.